HELOC Fundamentals

The Home Equity Wealth Series

By Joseph G. Correa

Licensed Mortgage Broker

Finibi Mortgage

Copyright & Legal Notice

First Edition, 2026

Table of Contents

Foreword

For decades, homeownership in America has been sold as a symbol of stability, success, and security, yet the single most powerful financial feature of owning a home has been almost completely ignored, misunderstood, or misused by most families: equity. Millions of homeowners faithfully make their monthly mortgage payments for thirty years, slowly building equity while believing that the only way to access that wealth is to sell their home or refinance it. This belief is not just incomplete—it is financially damaging. Equity is not just a number on a statement. It is a living financial asset, capable of funding businesses, paying off high-interest debt, financing investments, and creating generational wealth when used correctly. Yet because the system that teaches people how mortgages work is built to sell loans—not to build wealth—most homeowners are never shown how to use their equity safely, strategically, or intelligently. This book exists to correct that imbalance and to give homeowners the missing education that lenders, banks, and even financial advisors rarely provide.

A Home Equity Line of Credit, or HELOC, is one of the most misunderstood financial tools in modern finance. To some, it sounds risky. To others, it feels complicated. And to many, it is completely invisible. Yet for those who understand how it truly works, a HELOC can be one of the most flexible, low-cost, and powerful sources of capital available to everyday people. The same financial structure used by large corporations and wealthy investors to fund projects, control cash flow, and increase returns is available to homeowners who know how to access it properly. Unfortunately, without proper education, a HELOC can also be misused in ways that create stress, financial instability, and unnecessary risk. This is why this series begins not with strategies or investment tactics, but with fundamentals. Before you can use home equity to build wealth, eliminate debt, or grow a business, you must understand how it works at the most practical and technical level.

This series was written to do what banks and loan officers rarely do: tell the truth about how home equity really works. Most marketing materials focus on selling a loan, not on teaching a borrower how to use that loan responsibly over time. Borrowers are shown rates, payment examples, and closing costs, but they are not shown how credit lines cycle, how interest is calculated, how draws affect available credit, or how small decisions can dramatically change long-term outcomes. HELOCs are not dangerous. Misunderstood HELOCs are dangerous. Used correctly, a HELOC is one of the safest, most controlled forms of leverage available because it is backed by a real asset, structured as a revolving credit line, and typically carries far lower interest rates than credit cards, personal loans, or business financing. This book will remove the mystery, fear, and confusion so that you can make informed decisions based on knowledge rather than marketing.

As a licensed mortgage broker who has helped thousands of homeowners, real estate investors, business owners, and families access and use their home equity, I have seen firsthand how powerful this tool can be when it is used properly—and how damaging it can be when it is not. I have watched people eliminate six-figure credit card balances, fund business expansions, purchase rental properties, and create passive income streams using HELOCs. I have also seen borrowers struggle because no one taught them how to manage their credit line, how to structure their payments, or how to avoid common traps built into traditional lending systems. The difference between success and failure is almost never the HELOC itself. It is the level of education behind the borrower using it. This book is designed to give you that education.

You will not find hype in these pages. You will not find promises of quick riches or shortcuts to wealth. What you will find is clarity. You will learn how HELOCs are structured, how they differ from home equity loans and cash-out refinances, how lenders calculate risk, how credit limits are determined, and how interest is applied. You will learn why a HELOC is not just a loan, but a financial tool that behaves more like a credit card secured by real estate. You will understand why having access to capital is often more valuable than having cash sitting idle in a bank account. And you will begin to see your home not just as a place to live, but as a financial engine that can work for you instead of against you.

This book is the foundation of everything that follows in this series. Before you can qualify for a HELOC, invest with one, or use one to eliminate debt, you must understand the mechanics behind it. Just as a pilot must understand how an aircraft works before flying it, a homeowner must understand how a HELOC works before using it. Without that understanding, even the best financial tools can lead to poor outcomes. With it, even ordinary homeowners can achieve extraordinary financial control.

The modern economy has changed. Wages have not kept up with inflation. Traditional savings accounts no longer build meaningful wealth. And relying solely on retirement plans has become increasingly uncertain. In this environment, access to low-cost capital is one of the most important financial advantages a person can have. Your home is often your largest asset, yet for most people it remains financially dormant. A

HELOC gives you the ability to activate that asset without selling it. It gives you liquidity without liquidation. It gives you flexibility without surrendering ownership. When used responsibly, it allows you to move through financial opportunities with speed and control rather than hesitation and limitation.

Throughout this series, you will see how HELOCs can be used to pay off debt faster, fund real estate investments, start or scale businesses, protect cash flow, and create financial resilience. But it all starts here—with understanding. This first book will give you the vocabulary, concepts, and mental framework you need to evaluate every HELOC offer you encounter. It will allow you to spot bad terms, avoid traps, and structure your credit line in a way that aligns with your financial goals rather than undermining them.

This knowledge is not just for investors or high-net-worth individuals. It is for homeowners who want to take control of their financial future. It is for families who want to stop living paycheck to paycheck. It is for entrepreneurs who need access to capital without surrendering equity in their businesses. It is for retirees who want to turn home equity into income without selling their home. And it is for anyone who believes that financial freedom should be built on understanding rather than luck.

The Home Equity Wealth Series was written to give you the same financial clarity that banks, investors, and institutional borrowers use every day. Book 1 lays the groundwork. Everything that follows builds on what you will learn here. If you read this book carefully, you will never look at your mortgage, your home, or your financial options the same way again. Your house will no longer feel like a static asset. It will become a dynamic financial tool—one that, when used correctly, can open doors that once felt permanently closed.

Welcome to HELOC Fundamentals. This is where real financial control begins.

Chapter 1

What a HELOC Really Is

A Home Equity Line of Credit, commonly called a HELOC, is not a loan in the traditional sense. It is a revolving credit line secured by the equity in your home, meaning it behaves much more like a credit card than a mortgage. The key difference is that instead of being backed by your income alone, it is backed by the value of your property. This gives lenders greater security, which is why HELOCs typically come with far lower interest rates than unsecured debt such as credit cards, personal loans, or business loans. When you open a HELOC, the lender approves you for a maximum credit limit based on the amount of usable equity in your home, your credit profile, and the lender's internal risk guidelines. You do not receive that full amount in cash at closing. Instead, you receive access to a credit line that you can draw from, pay down, and reuse repeatedly over time.

This structure is what makes a HELOC so powerful. Unlike a traditional home equity loan, which gives you a lump sum and a fixed payment, a HELOC allows you to borrow only what you need, when you need it. If you have a $150,000 HELOC and only use $20,000, you are only charged interest on the $20,000 you actually borrowed. The remaining $130,000 remains available for future use. As you pay down the balance, your available credit increases again. This revolving feature allows homeowners to use their equity over and over without having to refinance or apply for new loans every time they need capital.

To understand why this matters, you must understand how equity works. Equity is the difference between what your home is worth and what you owe on your mortgage. If your home is worth $500,000 and your mortgage balance is $300,000, you have $200,000 in equity. Lenders do not allow you to borrow all of that equity. Most HELOC programs allow you to borrow up to a combined loan-to-value ratio, often called CLTV, of 80% to 90%. This means that the total of your mortgage balance plus your HELOC balance cannot exceed a certain percentage of the home's value. If a lender allows 80% CLTV on a $500,000 home, the maximum combined debt allowed is $400,000. If you already owe $300,000 on your first mortgage, that leaves up to $100,000 available for a HELOC.

Once the HELOC is opened, it has two phases: the draw period and the repayment period. The draw period is usually 5 to 10 years, during which you can borrow, repay, and re-borrow funds as needed. During this time, most HELOCs require only interest payments on the outstanding balance, though you are always allowed to pay principal as well. After the draw period ends, the HELOC enters the repayment period, usually lasting 10 to 20 years. At that point, the balance is amortized and you begin making principal and interest payments until the balance is paid off. Understanding this timeline is critical because it affects cash flow, long-term cost, and financial planning.

Interest on a HELOC is usually variable, meaning it can change over time based on an index such as the prime rate. This scares many borrowers, but what most do not realize is that HELOC rates are still usually far lower than credit cards or personal loans, even when rates rise. More importantly, because a HELOC is revolving, you have control over how much interest you pay. The faster you pay down the balance, the less interest you accrue. Unlike fixed mortgages, where you are locked into decades of scheduled interest, a HELOC allows you to actively manage and minimize your interest costs.

Another major advantage of a HELOC is liquidity. Liquidity means access to money when you need it. A homeowner with $150,000 sitting in home equity but no HELOC has zero liquidity. That equity cannot be accessed quickly without selling the home or refinancing, both of which take time, paperwork, and often thousands of dollars in fees. A homeowner with a HELOC already in place has instant access to capital. That means if a business opportunity appears, a property becomes available, or an emergency occurs, the funds are already there. Because a HELOC is secured by your home, it must be used responsibly. This does not mean it should be feared. It means it should be managed. Just like a business line of credit, a HELOC is a financial tool. Used to fund consumption and depreciating items, it can create problems. Used to replace high-interest debt, invest in income-producing assets, or improve cash flow, it can dramatically improve financial stability. The key is understanding that the HELOC itself is not the risk. Misuse of leverage is the risk.

Most people are taught to avoid debt, but wealthy individuals are taught to control it. A HELOC allows homeowners to convert dead equity into active capital. It allows money to move instead of sit still. It allows households to operate with the same financial flexibility that banks and corporations use every day. Once you understand this, you stop asking whether a HELOC is good or bad and start asking whether it is being used intelligently.

Practical Example: *How a HELOC Works in Real Life*

Imagine a homeowner named Lisa who owns a home worth $500,000. Her existing mortgage balance is $300,000. This means Lisa has $200,000 in equity. Her lender allows a maximum combined loan-to-value of 80%. Eighty percent of $500,000 is $400,000. That means the lender will allow

Lisa's total mortgage plus HELOC balances to go up to $400,000. Since she already owes $300,000, she can qualify for a HELOC of up to $100,000. The bank approves her for a $100,000 HELOC with a variable interest rate of 8% and a 10-year draw period.

Lisa does not receive $100,000 in her bank account. Instead, she receives access to a $100,000 credit line. She decides to use $30,000 to pay off credit cards that were charging 22% interest. When she draws $30,000 from the HELOC, her HELOC balance becomes $30,000 and her available credit becomes $70,000. The interest on her HELOC is calculated only on the $30,000 she borrowed. At 8% interest, the annual interest is $2,400, which is $200 per month. Previously, her $30,000 in credit card debt was costing her $6,600 per year in interest. By moving that debt to the HELOC, she saves $4,200 per year in interest.

Lisa continues making the same $800 per month she was paying on her credit cards, but now she applies it to her HELOC. Each month, $200 goes to interest and $600 goes to principal. After one month, her HELOC balance drops from $30,000 to $29,400. Her available credit increases to $70,600. After one year, she has paid down approximately $7,200 in principal, reducing her HELOC balance to about $22,800 and increasing her available credit to $77,200. Now

Lisa decides to use $50,000 from her HELOC to buy a small rental property. She draws $50,000, bringing her total HELOC balance to $72,800. Her available credit drops to $27,200. The rental property generates $800 per month in net cash flow. Lisa uses that $800 to pay down the HELOC. At 8% interest, the monthly interest on $72,800 is about $485. That means $315 of each payment goes toward principal. Over one year, she reduces the balance by about $3,780 while her tenant effectively pays down her debt.

After three years, Lisa has paid off most of the original credit card balance and a significant portion of the rental property funding. Her HELOC balance drops to $55,000. Her available credit increases to $45,000. She now has more borrowing power than she started with, even though she has invested in real estate and eliminated high-interest debt. This is the power of a revolving credit line secured by a real asset.

Because Lisa only pays interest on what she uses, and because she continuously pays down the balance, she controls her risk. If she had taken a $100,000 home equity loan instead, she would have paid interest on the full $100,000 whether she needed it or not. With the HELOC, she paid interest only on what she used, when she used it.

This example shows that a HELOC is not just a loan. It is a

financial system. It allows homeowners to move money from expensive debt to cheap debt, from idle equity to productive assets, and from stagnant finances to dynamic growth. When used with discipline, basic math, and a clear plan, a HELOC becomes one of the most powerful tools a homeowner can use to build financial freedom.

Chapter 2

How HELOC Limits, Rates, and Payments Really Work

A HELOC is only as powerful as the structure behind it. Most borrowers focus on how much money they can access, but the real control lies in how the credit line is calculated, how interest is applied, and how payments affect available credit over time. When you understand these three elements—limits, rates, and payments—you gain the ability to predict exactly how your HELOC will behave before you ever draw a dollar. This allows you to avoid surprises, manage risk, and design your financial strategy around facts rather than guesses.

HELOC limits are based on a formula called combined loan-to-value, or CLTV. This formula measures how much of your home's value is being used as collateral by all loans attached to the property. If a lender allows 85 percent CLTV and your home is worth $600,000, the maximum total debt allowed on the home is $510,000. If your first mortgage balance is $350,000, that leaves up to $160,000 available for a HELOC. This limit does not mean you must use the full amount. It simply defines the ceiling of how much the lender is willing to secure against the property. The unused portion is risk-free because no interest is charged on money that is not borrowed.

Interest on a HELOC is calculated daily based on the outstanding balance. Most HELOCs use a variable rate tied to the prime rate plus a margin set by the lender. For example, if prime is 8.5 percent and the lender adds a margin of 1 percent, the HELOC rate becomes 9.5 percent. If prime rises or falls, the HELOC rate adjusts accordingly. This means HELOC payments change over time, but it also means that when rates drop, the borrower benefits immediately without refinancing. Because interest is charged only on the outstanding balance, controlling how much you borrow and how fast you repay directly controls how much interest you pay.

During the draw period, HELOCs usually require interest-only payments. This means your minimum payment covers only the interest that accrued during that month. If you borrowed $50,000 at 9 percent, your monthly interest would be about $375. That is your required payment. If you pay only that amount, the balance does not decrease. If you pay more than that, the extra goes directly to principal, reducing the balance and increasing your available credit. This feature allows borrowers to manage cash flow while still retaining the ability to aggressively pay down debt when possible.

Payments on a HELOC behave differently than payments on a mortgage. With a mortgage, your payment is fixed and your balance declines slowly at first because most of the payment goes to interest. With a HELOC, you choose how fast the balance declines. If you make only the minimum payment, the balance stays the same. If you double the payment, the balance falls quickly. This gives the borrower direct control over both risk and cost. The faster the balance is reduced, the more credit becomes available again and the less interest is paid over time.

Because HELOCs are revolving, they act like financial engines. When money flows in, the balance goes down. When money flows out, the balance goes up. Understanding this cycle allows you to design strategies where income, investments, or savings continuously refill your available credit. This is why HELOCs are so effective for debt elimination, investing, and cash flow management. The borrower is no longer trapped in fixed schedules or rigid loan structures. Instead, the borrower is operating a flexible credit system backed by a hard asset.

The biggest mistake borrowers make is treating a HELOC like free money. It is not. It is borrowed money secured by your home. But it is also one of the cheapest, most flexible sources of capital most homeowners will ever have access to. When used with discipline, it allows you to move faster, reduce interest costs, and make better financial decisions because you are no longer constrained by cash shortages. Once you understand how limits, rates, and payments interact, you stop guessing and start calculating. Every draw, every payment, and every financial move becomes predictable. That predictability is what turns a HELOC from a risk into a tool.

Practical Example: *How Limits, Rates, and Payments Work in Real Numbers*

Let's say Mark owns a home worth $600,000. His mortgage balance is $360,000. His lender allows 85 percent CLTV. Eighty-five percent of $600,000 is $510,000. When we subtract Mark's $360,000 mortgage, we find that he qualifies for a HELOC of up to $150,000. The lender approves him for that amount with a variable rate of 9 percent.

Mark initially uses $40,000 from the HELOC to renovate his home. His HELOC balance becomes $40,000, and his available credit becomes $110,000. At 9 percent interest, the annual interest on $40,000 is $3,600, which equals $300 per month. That is his minimum payment. If Mark pays only $300, his balance stays at $40,000. If he pays $600, then $300 goes to interest and $300 reduces the balance to $39,700.

Chapter 3

How HELOCs Are Used by Banks, Investors, and Smart Homeowners

A HELOC is not a consumer product. It is a capital access system. Banks, corporations, and professional investors do not rely on savings accounts to operate. They rely on revolving credit. This allows them to deploy money when opportunities appear, pull capital back when risk rises, and continuously reuse the same dollars to generate returns. A HELOC gives homeowners access to the same system, using their home as the asset that secures the credit line. Once you understand this, you stop thinking like a borrower and start thinking like a capital manager.

Most people are taught to save money first and then spend it. Wealth builders operate in reverse. They secure credit first and then let income and cash flow refill it. This allows them to move quickly when a property, business, or financial opportunity appears. If someone with a HELOC sees a discounted home, a distressed business, or a debt-payoff opportunity, they do not need to apply for a loan, wait for underwriting, or liquidate investments. They already have the capital ready. This speed is one of the most important financial advantages in the modern economy.

Banks use revolving credit lines internally for the same reason. A bank may lend out $100 million in the morning and receive loan payments and deposits back in the afternoon. The same dollars move in and out continuously. The goal is not to eliminate debt. The goal is to keep capital moving efficiently while minimizing interest and risk. A HELOC allows homeowners to do this on a smaller scale.

Investors use HELOCs to avoid selling assets. Selling a property or investment creates taxes, fees, and lost future growth. Borrowing against an asset allows them to access cash without giving up ownership. This is why real estate investors use HELOCs to fund down payments, renovations, and acquisitions. When the new investment produces income, it repays the HELOC, restoring the credit line for future use.

Smart homeowners use HELOCs to restructure their entire financial life. Instead of carrying credit card debt at 20 to 30 percent interest, they move it to a HELOC at a fraction of the cost. Instead of letting savings earn little interest, they let the HELOC provide liquidity and let their money stay invested. Instead of being trapped by fixed mortgage schedules, they use the HELOC as a cash-flow control tool.

The most powerful feature of a HELOC is not the interest rate. It is the ability to recycle capital. When you borrow, repay, and reborrow, the same equity can be used multiple times to generate value. This is how one dollar of equity can fund ten or twenty dollars of economic activity over time without increasing long-term risk.

When people misuse HELOCs, it is usually because they spend the money on things that do not create income or reduce debt. When people use HELOCs correctly, they use them to convert high-interest debt into low-interest debt, or to create assets that produce cash flow. The HELOC itself is neutral. It is the strategy behind it that determines the outcome.

Understanding how professionals use revolving credit changes how you see your home. It is no longer just shelter. It is a financial instrument. Once you learn to manage it properly, your house becomes one of the most powerful wealth-building tools you own.

Practical Example: *Using a HELOC the Way Professionals Do*

Let's look at a homeowner named Daniel. His home is worth $700,000. His mortgage balance is $420,000. His lender allows 85 percent CLTV. Eighty-five percent of $700,000 is $595,000. Subtracting his mortgage, Daniel qualifies for a HELOC of up to $175,000. Daniel opens the HELOC but does not immediately use it. This costs him nothing. He simply has access to $175,000 if needed. Six months later, Daniel finds a small duplex selling for $300,000. It needs $40,000 in repairs. The bank requires a $60,000 down payment. Daniel draws $100,000 from his HELOC to cover the down payment and repairs.

His HELOC balance becomes $100,000 and his available credit becomes $75,000. At 9 percent interest, his monthly HELOC interest is about $750. After renovations, the duplex rents for $3,000 per month. After expenses, it produces $1,200 in net cash flow. Daniel applies that $1,200 to the HELOC. $750 covers interest and $450 reduces the balance.

After one year, Daniel pays $14,400 into the HELOC. About $9,000 went to interest and $5,400 reduced principal. His HELOC balance drops to $94,600. His available credit increases to $80,400. The property also increases in value to $340,000.

After three years, Daniel's HELOC balance falls to $85,000. His available credit grows to $90,000. He now has more borrowing power than when he started, even though he used $100,000 to buy a rental property. He can now use the HELOC again to buy another property, repeating the cycle.

This is how investors build portfolios without constantly injecting new cash. The HELOC acts as a reusable capital engine. Every time an investment produces income or equity, it refills the credit line. Over time, one HELOC can fund multiple properties, businesses, or financial strategies.

Daniel never sold his home. He never refinanced. He never locked in a new long-term loan. He simply used his equity as revolving capital. This is how banks and investors think about money. A HELOC gives homeowners the same financial advantage when used correctly.

Chapter 4

How HELOCs Replace Traditional Savings and Emergency Funds

Most households are taught that financial security comes from saving cash. They are told to keep three to six months of expenses in a savings account in case something goes wrong. While this advice sounds responsible, it is financially inefficient in a modern economy. Cash sitting in a bank earns little interest while inflation steadily erodes its purchasing power. At the same time, families who lock up large amounts of money in savings often struggle with cash flow and are forced to use high-interest credit cards when emergencies occur. A HELOC provides a more powerful and flexible safety system because it allows homeowners to keep their money working while still maintaining instant access to capital.

A HELOC functions as a private emergency reserve backed by your home instead of by idle cash. When you open a HELOC, you create a pool of available credit that costs nothing until you use it. If your furnace breaks, medical bills arrive, or income drops temporarily, you can draw from the HELOC instead of draining savings or using high-interest debt. Because HELOC interest rates are far lower than credit cards, this immediately reduces the cost of emergencies. When income stabilizes, you simply pay the balance back and restore your available credit.

This system also allows your cash to stay invested or productive. Instead of keeping $50,000 in a savings account earning 1 to 2 percent, you can let that money earn 6, 8, or 10 percent through investments, business use, or even debt reduction while the HELOC stands ready as your safety net. The HELOC becomes your liquidity. Your cash becomes your growth engine. This separation is what wealthy households use to grow faster while taking less risk.

Traditional emergency funds force people to choose between safety and growth. HELOC-based liquidity allows them to have both. Because the credit line is secured by real estate, it is stable and long-term. Because it is revolving, it can be used, repaid, and reused endlessly. Because it is interest-based only when drawn, there is no penalty for simply having it available.

This is not about spending recklessly. It is about creating a smarter financial buffer. When your safety net is a HELOC, you never feel forced to sell investments, miss opportunities, or panic during financial stress. You already have capital access. That peace of mind is one of the most underrated benefits of having a HELOC in place.

Practical Example: *Using a HELOC Instead of a Savings Account*

Sarah owns a home worth $550,000. Her mortgage balance is $330,000. Her lender allows 80 percent CLTV. Eighty percent of $550,000 is $440,000. That means she qualifies for a HELOC of up to $110,000. She opens the HELOC but does not use it.

Sarah currently keeps $40,000 in a savings account earning 2 percent. That earns her $800 per year. Instead, she moves $30,000 into an investment earning 8 percent. That earns $2,400 per year. The difference is $1,600 in additional income.

Six months later, Sarah's air conditioning system fails and costs $10,000 to replace. Instead of withdrawing from savings, she draws $10,000 from her HELOC. At 8.5 percent interest, her monthly interest is about $71. Her investment continues earning money while she pays down the HELOC at $500 per month.

After one year, she has paid off the $10,000. Her HELOC balance returns to zero. Her available credit is again $110,000. Her investment earned more than the interest cost. Her cash never stopped working.

This is how a HELOC replaces traditional emergency funds. Instead of storing money in low-yield accounts, homeowners use their equity as a financial buffer while their cash grows. Over time, this strategy produces more wealth with less stress.

Chapter 5

How HELOCs Interact With Credit Scores, Risk, and Lender Behavior

Most borrowers think credit scores determine whether they qualify for a HELOC. In reality, credit scores only open the door. What lenders truly care about is risk. A HELOC is secured by your home, but the lender is still lending you a revolving credit line that can be used, repaid, and used again. This makes HELOC underwriting more sensitive than traditional mortgages. To understand how to qualify for the best terms and how to protect your borrowing power, you must understand how lenders view your credit profile, debt load, and financial behavior.

Credit scores are used as a filter. Higher scores reduce the lender's perception of risk and result in higher credit limits, lower interest rates, and better terms. Lower scores do not necessarily prevent approval, but they usually reduce the amount of equity a lender will allow you to access. This is because HELOCs are second-position loans. If a homeowner defaults, the first mortgage gets paid first. The HELOC lender takes more risk, so they rely heavily on credit quality to protect themselves. Debt-to-income ratio also plays a major role. Lenders calculate how much of your monthly income is already committed to debt. Even if you have high equity, too much existing debt can reduce or eliminate your HELOC approval. This is why many borrowers are surprised when they are told they qualify for less than expected. The HELOC is not limited by equity alone. It is limited by the lender's confidence that you can manage additional credit responsibly.

HELOC utilization also affects your credit score. Because HELOCs are revolving accounts, they impact your credit the same way credit cards do. If you use a large percentage of your available credit, your score may temporarily drop. When you pay the balance down, your score improves again. This is not a problem. It is part of how the system works. Smart borrowers understand that credit scores fluctuate and are managed through cash flow and balance control.

Lenders also look at how HELOCs are used. Borrowers who consistently max out their lines and make only minimum payments appear riskier. Borrowers who use credit strategically and pay down balances quickly are rewarded with higher limits, lower rates, and better future approvals. In other words, how you use your HELOC determines how lenders treat you.

Understanding these mechanics allows you to use a HELOC without damaging your financial profile. It also allows you to structure your debt in a way that improves your long-term creditworthiness rather than harming it. When used correctly, a HELOC can actually strengthen your credit profile by replacing high-interest debt, reducing utilization, and improving cash flow stability.

Practical Example: *How HELOC Usage Impacts Credit and Borrowing Power*

Michael owns a home worth $650,000 with a $390,000 mortgage. He qualifies for a HELOC of $160,000. His credit score is 760. He opens the HELOC but only uses $20,000 to pay off credit cards.

His credit card balances drop from $20,000 to zero. His HELOC balance is $20,000. His utilization on credit cards goes to zero, improving his credit score. Even though his HELOC is at 12.5 percent utilization, his overall profile improves. His score rises to 780.

Michael then pays $1,000 per month on the HELOC. The interest at 9 percent is $150. That means $850 goes to principal. After one year, he has paid off over $10,000. His HELOC balance drops to under $10,000. His available credit is now over $150,000.

Because Michael used the HELOC responsibly, his lender increases his credit limit to $200,000. He now has more borrowing power than before. His credit score is higher, his debt is cheaper, and his financial risk is lower.

This example shows that HELOCs do not damage credit when used correctly. They strengthen it.

Chapter 6

How HELOCs Create Long-Term Wealth Through Capital Recycling

The greatest power of a HELOC is not that it lets you borrow money. It is that it lets you reuse the same money over and over without selling assets or locking yourself into permanent debt. This concept is called capital recycling. Banks, hedge funds, and wealthy investors rely on it to grow faster with less risk. A HELOC allows homeowners to use the same principle using their home as the underlying asset.

When you use a HELOC to fund something that produces income or equity, that investment begins paying the HELOC back. As the balance falls, your available credit rises. This means the same credit line becomes usable again. Each cycle allows you to deploy capital, recover it, and redeploy it. Over time, this creates exponential financial efficiency.

Traditional loans trap capital. You borrow a lump sum, pay it back over decades, and cannot reuse it without refinancing. A HELOC releases capital. You borrow, pay, and reuse without new underwriting or closing costs. This allows one pool of equity to fund multiple investments over time. This system also reduces risk. Because the balance is constantly falling as income flows in, you are never permanently locked into high debt. You maintain liquidity. You control exposure. You can stop borrowing at any time. This flexibility is what makes HELOC-based investing safer than fixed long-term leverage when done correctly.

Capital recycling works in three stages. First, you deploy capital. Second, the investment produces cash flow or equity. Third, that return refills your HELOC. This process repeats. Each cycle increases your net worth while keeping debt manageable.

This is how ordinary homeowners can create long-term wealth without needing large cash reserves. The HELOC becomes a renewable financial engine.

Practical Example: *How Capital Recycling Works With Real Numbers*

Tom owns a home worth $800,000. His mortgage balance is $480,000. His lender allows 85 percent CLTV. Eighty-five percent of $800,000 is $680,000. Subtracting his mortgage gives him a HELOC limit of $200,000.

Tom uses $100,000 from the HELOC to buy a rental property. His HELOC balance becomes $100,000. His available credit is $100,000. The interest at 8.5 percent is $708 per month. The rental generates $1,200 per month in net cash flow. Each month, Tom pays the $708 interest and applies the remaining $492 to principal. Over one year, he pays $5,904 in principal. His balance drops to $94,096. His available credit increases to $105,904.

Over three years, Tom pays down about $18,000 in principal. His HELOC balance drops to $82,000. His available credit increases to $118,000. The rental also appreciates by $40,000.

Tom now uses $80,000 from his HELOC to buy a second property. His HELOC balance rises to $162,000. His available credit drops to $38,000. The second property produces $900 per month in cash flow. Combined cash flow from both properties is now $2,100 per month.

At 8.5 percent, interest on $162,000 is $1,147 per month. That leaves $953 to pay down principal. Over one year, Tom pays off $11,436. His balance drops to $150,564. His available credit increases to $49,436.

This process continues. Each year, Tom's debt shrinks while his assets grow. The HELOC never stays maxed out. It constantly refills. The math works because income exceeds interest. This is capital recycling.

Over ten years, Tom owns multiple properties funded by the same $200,000 HELOC. His net worth increases while his borrowing power stays intact. This is how HELOCs create long-term wealth when used with discipline and basic math.

Chapter 7

How HELOCs Are Used to Eliminate Debt Faster Than Any Other Method

Most people spend decades trapped in consumer debt not because they borrow too much, but because they borrow at the wrong interest rate and with the wrong structure. Credit cards, personal loans, and auto loans are designed to keep balances high and payments slow. A HELOC changes this by allowing high-interest debt to be converted into low-interest, revolving credit that can be paid down aggressively. This is why HELOC-based debt elimination works even when traditional budgeting fails.

When you move debt from a credit card charging 24 percent to a HELOC charging 8 or 9 percent, the interest portion of every payment drops dramatically. That means more of your payment goes to principal. The faster principal falls, the less interest accrues. This creates a compounding effect where each payment becomes more powerful than the last. Over time, the same payment that once barely reduced debt begins to eliminate it rapidly.

The second advantage is cash flow control. A HELOC allows interest-only minimum payments. This gives borrowers flexibility when income fluctuates while still allowing them to make aggressive payments when possible. Unlike credit cards, HELOCs do not trap you in minimum-payment cycles that stretch for decades. You control the repayment speed.

The third advantage is revolving credit. As balances fall, available credit rises. This allows the HELOC to absorb new expenses or unexpected bills without creating new loans. Instead of going back to credit cards, homeowners continue using the HELOC, keeping all debt at low interest.

Debt elimination with a HELOC is not about spending more. It is about restructuring existing obligations into a system that works for you instead of against you. The math alone makes this approach powerful. But the psychological benefit of seeing balances drop faster creates momentum that changes financial behavior permanently.

Practical Example: *Eliminating Debt With HELOC Math*

Jessica owns a home worth $500,000. Her mortgage balance is $300,000. She qualifies for a HELOC of $100,000. She has $45,000 in credit card debt at 22 percent and $15,000 in personal loans at 14 percent. Her total high-interest debt is $60,000. Jessica uses $60,000 from her HELOC to pay off all high-interest debt. Her HELOC balance becomes $60,000. Her available credit is $40,000. The interest at 9 percent is

$450 per month. Previously, she was paying over $1,200 per month in minimum payments.

Jessica continues paying $1,200 per month, but now it goes to the HELOC. $450 covers interest. $750 goes to principal. In one year, she pays $9,000 in principal. Her balance drops to $51,000.

In the second year, interest drops because the balance is lower. Interest on $51,000 at 9 percent is about $383 per month. Now $817 of her $1,200 goes to principal. By the end of year two, she has paid off another $9,804. Her balance drops to $41,196.

By year three, her interest is only $309 per month. That means $891 goes to principal. After year three, her balance drops to about $30,500.

By year four, interest is $229 per month. That means $971 goes to principal. After year four, the balance drops to about $18,900.

By year five, interest is $142 per month. That means $1,058 goes to principal. After year five, the balance drops to about $6,200.

In year six, the HELOC is paid off. Jessica eliminated $60,000 of debt in just over five years using the same payment she was already making. She saved over $40,000 in interest compared to credit cards. Her HELOC is now available again for emergencies or opportunities.

This is how HELOC-based debt elimination works. Lower interest, faster principal reduction, and revolving credit create a system that naturally accelerates financial freedom.

Chapter 8

How HELOCs Turn Homes Into Wealth-Building Machines

Most homeowners believe their house is simply a place to live and a long-term retirement asset. In reality, a home is one of the most powerful financial engines a family can own. A HELOC is the mechanism that allows that engine to run. When equity is activated through a credit line, the home becomes a source of capital that can fund investments, businesses, debt elimination, and passive income. Without a HELOC, equity is trapped. With one, equity becomes a working asset.

The difference between a house that builds wealth and a house that simply sits is cash flow. When equity is used to acquire or create income-producing assets, that income pays down the HELOC, refills the credit line, and increases the homeowner's net worth. This creates a cycle where the home funds wealth, wealth pays back the home, and the homeowner's financial position strengthens year after year.

Unlike traditional investing, this approach does not require large savings. The HELOC provides the capital. The assets provide the return. The borrower manages the flow. This structure allows ordinary homeowners to operate like professional investors without needing institutional funding.

The key is that HELOC-funded investments must be cash-flow positive. If the income exceeds the interest cost, the system becomes self-sustaining. Over time, the HELOC balance falls while asset value rises. That is how wealth is created safely.

Practical Example: *Turning One Home Into a Wealth Engine*

David owns a home worth $750,000. His mortgage is $450,000. He qualifies for a $187,500 HELOC. He uses $150,000 to buy two rental properties.

His HELOC balance is $150,000. His interest at 8 percent is $1,000 per month. The two rentals produce $2,600 per month in net income.

David applies the full $2,600 to the HELOC. $1,000 covers interest. $1,600 reduces principal. Over one year, he pays $19,200 in principal. His balance drops to $130,800.

In year two, interest is lower. Interest on $130,800 is about $872 per month. That means $1,728 goes to principal. After year two, the balance drops to about $110,064.

By year five, the HELOC is almost paid off. David owns two cash-flowing properties funded by his home equity. His

HELOC becomes available again, allowing him to repeat the process.

This is how one home becomes a wealth machine when used with discipline and basic math.

Chapter 9

How to Use a HELOC Without Ever Putting Your Home at Risk

One of the most common fears homeowners have about using a HELOC is the idea that they could lose their home. This fear is not irrational, but it is misunderstood. The risk does not come from the HELOC itself. It comes from how it is used. When a HELOC is managed like a professional credit facility rather than a consumer loan, the risk to the home can actually be lower than carrying high-interest debt, unstable investments, or poor cash flow.

The first rule of protecting your home is never to use a HELOC for expenses that do not either reduce other debt or produce income. Using home equity for vacations, lifestyle spending, or depreciating purchases converts stable housing equity into fragile consumer debt. This is what creates danger. In contrast, using a HELOC to eliminate 20 percent interest debt or to fund a cash-flowing asset improves financial stability rather than weakening it.

The second rule is maintaining a safety buffer. Professional borrowers never use 100 percent of their credit lines. They leave unused capacity so they can handle emergencies, market changes, or temporary income drops. A HELOC should always have unused credit available. This protects you from needing to sell assets or miss payments when unexpected events occur.

The third rule is cash-flow coverage. Every dollar borrowed must have a clear repayment source. That source can be income, savings, investment returns, or rental cash flow. If there is no repayment plan, the HELOC becomes permanent debt. When there is a repayment plan, it becomes temporary leverage.

The fourth rule is rate management. HELOCs are usually variable. This means you must understand how rate changes affect your payments. Smart borrowers run the math at higher rates before borrowing. If the numbers still work when rates rise, the strategy is safe.

Risk management is not about avoiding leverage. It is about controlling it. A HELOC gives you more control than almost any other form of debt because it is revolving, flexible, and secured by a stable asset. When used with discipline, it can actually reduce financial risk by replacing dangerous debt and increasing liquidity.

Practical Example: *How Risk Is Controlled With Real Numbers*

Let's look at Angela. Her home is worth $700,000. Her mortgage is $420,000. She qualifies for a $140,000 HELOC. She decides to use $90,000 to pay off credit cards and invest in a rental property.

Her HELOC balance becomes $90,000. Her available credit remains $50,000. At 8.5 percent interest, her monthly interest is $637. She has $800 per month in cash flow from the rental and saves $600 per month from eliminated credit card payments. That gives her $1,400 per month to cover the HELOC.

After paying $637 in interest, she applies $763 to principal. In one year, she pays $9,156 in principal. Her balance drops to $80,844. Her available credit increases to $59,156.

If rates rise to 11 percent, her interest would become $741. Her cash flow still covers it. Because she left $50,000 unused and structured positive cash flow, Angela remains safe even when conditions change.

Over five years, Angela's HELOC balance falls below $50,000 while her rental property increases in value. Her home is safer than before because her debt is lower and her income is higher. This is how HELOC risk is managed with math, not fear.

Chapter 10

The Smart Borrower's HELOC Blueprint

A HELOC is not a product. It is a financial operating system. Most homeowners approach it like a loan, but the smartest borrowers use it as a blueprint for managing cash flow, debt, investment capital, and long-term risk. When structured properly, a HELOC allows a household to control money instead of being controlled by it. This chapter ties together everything you have learned and shows how to design a HELOC strategy that works in every stage of life.

The first step of the blueprint is securing the maximum possible credit line while keeping your risk low. This means applying when your credit score is high, your income is strong, and your debt is low. Even if you do not need the money now, opening a HELOC when you qualify gives you long-term access to capital that may not be available later. A HELOC costs nothing when unused, but it becomes priceless when opportunities or emergencies arise.

The second step is structuring the HELOC as your primary financial buffer. Instead of relying on large savings accounts or high-limit credit cards, you use the HELOC as your liquidity. Your cash can then be invested, used to reduce debt, or deployed into assets that grow. This keeps your money productive while your safety net stays intact.

The third step is converting bad debt into good debt. High-interest credit cards, personal loans, and car notes drain wealth. A HELOC replaces those with a single low-interest line that can be paid down aggressively. This alone can save tens of thousands of dollars in interest and shorten the time it takes to become debt-free.

The fourth step is controlled investment. Once your financial foundation is stable, the HELOC becomes your capital source for income-producing assets. Because it is revolving, every dollar returned restores your borrowing power. This allows you to scale without increasing permanent debt.

The fifth step is constant risk management. You always keep unused credit, positive cash flow, and a plan for higher rates. This makes your HELOC strategy resilient in any market.

This blueprint allows a homeowner to move from survival to control, from control to growth, and from growth to financial independence.

Practical Example: *The HELOC Blueprint in Action*

Let's look at Brian. His home is worth $800,000. His mortgage balance is $480,000. His lender allows 85 percent

CLTV. That gives him a total allowable debt of $680,000. Subtracting his mortgage leaves him with a HELOC of $200,000.

Brian opens the HELOC but only uses $50,000 to pay off credit cards and a car loan. His HELOC balance is $50,000. His available credit is $150,000. At 8.5 percent interest, his monthly interest is about $354. He was previously paying $1,200 per month on those debts, so he applies that same amount to the HELOC.

Each month, $354 goes to interest and $846 goes to principal. In one year, Brian pays off about $10,152. His balance drops to $39,848. His available credit increases to $160,152.

In year two, Brian uses $80,000 from the HELOC to buy a rental property. His HELOC balance rises to $119,848. His available credit falls to $80,152. The rental produces $1,100 per month in net income. Brian applies that to the HELOC.

Interest at 8.5 percent on $119,848 is about $849 per month. That leaves $251 going to principal. Combined with the $1,200 he already pays, Brian now pays $2,300 per month. Of that, about $1,451 goes to principal.

After one year, he reduces the HELOC balance by about $17,412. His balance drops to $102,436. His available credit increases to $97,564. By year five, Brian has eliminated consumer debt and owns a rental property. His HELOC balance is under $60,000. His available credit is over $140,000. His home equity is higher than when he started. His income is higher. His risk is lower.

This is the HELOC blueprint. One home, one credit line, disciplined math, and a long-term strategy transform ordinary homeownership into financial independence.

Chapter 11

How to Scale, Optimize, and Future-Proof a HELOC Strategy

Once a homeowner understands how to use a HELOC safely, eliminate debt, and create income, the next stage is optimization. At this level, the HELOC stops being a simple credit line and becomes a financial platform. The goal is no longer just to borrow and repay, but to continuously increase borrowing power, reduce risk, and create long-term resilience regardless of what happens in the economy.

The first element of scaling is equity growth. Every payment you make on your mortgage, every HELOC dollar you pay down, and every increase in your home's value increases your usable equity. This means your borrowing capacity grows over time. Smart borrowers periodically re-evaluate their HELOC limits and request increases or open second HELOCs when allowed. This expands liquidity without adding permanent debt.

The second element is rate optimization. HELOCs are variable, but many lenders allow fixed-rate sub-accounts. Borrowers can lock portions of their balance when rates are low and leave other portions floating. This creates a blended rate that reduces volatility while maintaining flexibility.

The third element is cash-flow layering. Instead of relying on one income source, professional HELOC users build multiple streams that all feed into the credit line. Salary, rental income, business income, and investment returns all flow into the HELOC, accelerating principal reduction and restoring available credit faster.

The fourth element is downside protection. Advanced borrowers maintain liquidity buffers, unused credit, and conservative draw levels. They stress-test their numbers at higher rates and lower income levels. This ensures the strategy survives recessions, market crashes, and job changes.

This level of HELOC mastery transforms a household into a financial fortress.

Practical Example: *Scaling and Future-Proofing With Real Numbers*

Let's look at Maria. Her home is worth $900,000. Her mortgage is $500,000. She qualifies for a $265,000 HELOC. She has $120,000 drawn for investments. Her interest at 8.5 percent is $850 per month.

Her rentals and business generate $3,500 per month in net

cash flow. She applies all of it to the HELOC. After paying interest, $2,650 goes to principal. Over one year, she pays off $31,800. Her balance drops to $88,200. Her available credit increases to $176,800.

Maria locks $50,000 into a fixed-rate sub-account at 6.5 percent. The rest floats. This lowers her overall rate. Her blended interest drops to about $600 per month. Now more cash flow goes to principal.

Over three years, Maria eliminates the HELOC balance while growing her income streams. Her available credit reaches $265,000. Her home value increases to $1 million. She now qualifies for a larger HELOC, increasing her capital base without increasing risk.

Even if rates rise or income dips, Maria has unused credit, positive cash flow, and a paid-down balance. Her home is safer than before. This is how HELOC strategies scale safely over decades.

Chapter 12

The Lifetime Home Equity Strategy

Most financial plans are built around income and savings. Very few are built around assets. Your home is not just shelter. It is a permanent capital base. When structured correctly, it becomes a financial partner that supports you for life. A HELOC is the mechanism that allows this to happen. This chapter shows how to design a lifetime home equity strategy that adapts as your income, goals, and stage of life change.

In your early earning years, the HELOC is used primarily to eliminate bad debt and build liquidity. In your peak earning years, it is used to fund investments, businesses, and asset acquisition. In your later years, it becomes a tax-efficient income stream and a financial stabilizer. This evolution allows you to use the same home to support multiple decades of financial growth.

The key is never to let equity sit idle. Equity that is not producing income is losing value to inflation. Equity that is safely deployed through a HELOC is creating opportunity. When managed correctly, the balance rises and falls, but your net worth grows. The lifetime strategy is built on three principles: liquidity, leverage control, and income replacement. Liquidity ensures you never run out of money. Leverage control ensures you never risk the home. Income replacement ensures that when work ends, cash flow continues.

A HELOC allows homeowners to access capital without selling or refinancing. This means you never have to liquidate your home to access its value. You can live in it, borrow against it, repay it, and borrow again. This is what makes the home a permanent financial engine.

Practical Example: *A 30-Year Home Equity Wealth Plan*

James buys a home for $600,000. Over 10 years, it appreciates to $850,000. His mortgage drops to $420,000. He qualifies for a HELOC of $260,000.

He uses $80,000 to eliminate debt and $100,000 to buy two rentals. His HELOC balance is $180,000. At 8 percent, interest is $1,200 per month. Rentals produce $2,800 per month. After interest, $1,600 goes to principal.

Over five years, James pays down $96,000. His balance drops to $84,000. His available credit increases to $176,000.

By year 20, his mortgage is nearly paid off. His home is worth $1.2 million. His HELOC limit rises to $600,000. He uses it to fund income-producing assets that replace his salary. At retirement, James uses a small HELOC draw each year instead of selling investments, keeping taxes low. His home continues to support his lifestyle.

This is how one home becomes a lifetime financial partner through disciplined HELOC use and basic math.

In year two, she uses $60,000 from the HELOC to buy a third rental. Her balance rises to $192,796. Interest becomes $1,366. Cash flow rises to $4,300. After interest, $2,934 goes to principal.

Over three years, Laura's HELOC balance drops below $100,000 while she owns three rentals and a business. Her income streams are paying down her debt faster than she can borrow it.

This is how one HELOC supports multiple assets while keeping the home protected through cash-flow-driven repayment.

Chapter 14

How to Grow Aggressively While Keeping Your Home Safe

The difference between amateurs and professionals in any financial system is not how much they earn, but how well they control risk. A HELOC can accelerate wealth, but only if it is used with disciplined structure. This chapter explains how to grow aggressively while still keeping your home safer every year.

The first principle is margin of safety. Professional borrowers never operate at the limit of their credit. Even if a HELOC is $300,000, they may only use $150,000. This gives them room to absorb market changes, interest rate increases, and income fluctuations without stress.

The second principle is cash-flow dominance. Every dollar borrowed must be backed by reliable income that exceeds interest costs. If income disappears, borrowing stops. If income grows, borrowing can expand. This keeps the HELOC self-regulating.

The third principle is diversification. One investment can fail. Five rarely do. HELOC strategies work best when capital is spread across multiple properties, businesses, or income streams that all feed the credit line.

The fourth principle is draw timing. Smart borrowers draw money only when returns are locked in. They do not borrow in anticipation of income. They borrow once the deal is structured.

When these principles are followed, the home becomes more secure even while equity is being used.

Practical Example: *Aggressive Growth Without Risking the Home*

Chris owns a home worth $1,000,000. His mortgage is $550,000. He qualifies for a $300,000 HELOC. He limits himself to using no more than $150,000.

He uses $120,000 to buy two rentals. His HELOC balance is $120,000. At 8 percent interest, his payment is $800 per month. The rentals produce $2,400 per month in net cash flow.

After interest, $1,600 goes to principal. Over one year, he pays down $19,200. His balance drops to $100,800. His available credit rises to $199,200.

In year two, he uses $80,000 to buy another property. His balance rises to $180,800. Cash flow increases to $3,500. Interest becomes $1,205. That leaves $2,295 for principal.

After two more years, his balance drops below $120,000 again. Even though he keeps expanding, his risk remains low because income outpaces interest.

Chris is growing fast, but his home is safer than before. That is what disciplined HELOC leverage looks like.

Chapter 15

How to Turn a HELOC Into a Permanent Family Wealth Engine

The final stage of HELOC mastery is when the credit line stops being something you think about and starts becoming something your family relies on for decades. At this level, the HELOC is no longer just a financial tool. It is a family banking system. Just like wealthy families have trusts, holding companies, and private banks, a properly structured HELOC turns a home into a permanent source of capital, liquidity, and income for generations.

The key to making this work is separation of use and ownership. The home remains the anchor. The HELOC is the financial interface. The income-producing assets—real estate, businesses, investments—are the engines that repay and grow the system. As long as cash flow flows back into the HELOC, the family's borrowing power and net worth expand together.

This system is self-reinforcing. As assets grow, income increases. As income increases, the HELOC is paid down faster. As the HELOC is paid down, available credit increases. That increased credit is then used to acquire more assets. Over time, the family owns more income streams, more equity, and more financial flexibility while carrying less risk relative to net worth.

The family also gains financial resilience. Emergencies no longer require selling assets or going into panic mode. The HELOC provides liquidity. Investments remain intact. Taxes remain minimized. The household becomes financially shock-resistant.

At this level, the HELOC replaces savings accounts, emergency funds, business loans, and even retirement income. It becomes the private bank that funds education, opportunities, investments, and life itself.

Practical Example: *A 30-Year Family HELOC Wealth Engine*

Robert and Elena own a home worth $1,200,000. Their mortgage is $600,000. They qualify for a $420,000 HELOC. They begin by using $150,000 to eliminate debt and buy two rental properties.

Their HELOC balance is $150,000. At 8 percent, interest is $1,000 per month. Their rentals produce $3,200 per month in net income. After interest, $2,200 goes to principal. Over one year, they pay $26,400. Their balance drops to $123,600. Over five years, they pay down $132,000. Their balance falls to under $20,000. Their available credit grows to over $400,000. Their rentals appreciate and their income rises.

They then use the HELOC to fund college for their children and additional investments. Those investments repay the HELOC. By year 20, their mortgage is gone. Their home is worth over $2 million. Their HELOC limit exceeds $1 million.

They use small HELOC draws instead of selling assets in retirement, keeping taxes low. Their children inherit a home, income streams, and a credit system that funds opportunity.

This is how a HELOC becomes a permanent family wealth engine through disciplined math, smart cash flow, and generational strategy.

Final Thoughts

By the time you reach this point in *HELOC Fundamentals*, you no longer see your home the way most people do. What once felt like a static place to live now stands revealed as something far more powerful: a financial asset capable of generating opportunity, stability, and long-term wealth when used with intelligence and discipline. That shift in perception is the most important outcome of this book. The numbers, the formulas, and the strategies all matter, but they only work when you stop thinking like a borrower and start thinking like a steward of capital.

A Home Equity Line of Credit is not about going into debt. It is about gaining access. Access to liquidity. Access to opportunity. Access to flexibility. In a world where cash flow disruptions, rising costs, and unexpected events are normal, access to low-cost capital is one of the most valuable forms of financial security you can have. Most families live at the mercy of their next paycheck or their next credit card statement. A homeowner with a properly structured HELOC lives in a very different reality. They have options. They have breathing room. They have the ability to act instead of react. Throughout this book, you have seen how a HELOC replaces the traditional idea of saving with something far more dynamic. Instead of parking money in low-yield accounts while carrying high-interest debt, you use your equity as a financial buffer and let your cash stay productive. Instead of fearing emergencies, you design for them. Instead of hoping nothing goes wrong, you plan for when something does. This is how financial professionals think. And now, it is how you think.

You have also seen that leverage itself is not the enemy. Uncontrolled leverage is. A HELOC gives you more control over your borrowing than almost any other financial tool. You choose when to draw. You choose how much to repay. You choose how fast or slow to move. When this control is combined with discipline and positive cash flow, leverage becomes a stabilizer rather than a threat. It replaces chaos with structure and replaces financial stress with predictability.

One of the most powerful lessons of this book is that wealth is not built by how much you earn, but by how well you move money. Two households can make the same income and live completely different financial lives based on how they structure their cash flow, their debt, and their access to capital. A HELOC allows you to shift from a rigid, paycheck-dependent model into a flexible, capital-driven one. This is the same shift that separates consumers from investors and workers from owners. As you move forward, the most important thing to remember is that the HELOC is not the strategy. It is the platform. The strategy comes from what you choose to do with it. You can use it to eliminate debt. You can use it to build income. You can use it to create security for your family. Or you can misuse it and create stress. The difference is not the credit line. It is the clarity behind the decisions you make.

The goal is not to use every dollar of equity. The goal is to use equity intelligently. This means maintaining buffers, respecting cash flow, and always understanding how interest, payments, and income interact. When you do this, your home becomes safer over time, not riskier. Your equity grows. Your options expand. And your financial life becomes increasingly resilient to whatever the world throws at you.

What makes this approach so powerful is that it is not tied to a single market, a single job, or a single investment. It adapts. In good times, your HELOC helps you grow faster. In bad times, it helps you survive without panic. In retirement, it becomes a source of tax-efficient liquidity. At every stage of life, it remains useful. That is why it is not just a loan. It is a lifetime financial tool.

This book has given you the foundation. You now understand how HELOCs are structured, how interest works, how risk is controlled, and how capital can be recycled. You are no longer dependent on marketing slogans or fear-based advice. You can evaluate offers, run the math, and make decisions based on logic instead of emotion. That alone puts you ahead of the vast majority of homeowners.

But this is only the beginning. In the next books of *The Home Equity Wealth Series*, you will learn how to qualify for the best HELOCs, how to use them as an investor, how self-employed borrowers unlock them, how credit scores and underwriting really work, and how to structure advanced strategies for debt elimination, business funding, and wealth creation. Each book builds on the foundation you have just created.

Financial freedom is not built in a single move. It is built through systems that work over time. A HELOC is one of the most powerful systems a homeowner can have. Used correctly, it turns your home into a partner in your financial life rather than just a place you pay for every month.

You now know how it works. What you do with that knowledge is what will determine your future.

How to Get a Personalized HELOC Review

If you found *HELOC Fundamentals: How Home Equity Lines of Credit Really Work – and How to Use Them Safely* helpful, you may want to see how these concepts apply to your own home, credit profile, and financial goals. Every homeowner's situation is unique. Home value, mortgage balance, credit history, income type, and state-specific lending rules all affect how much equity you can access, what type of HELOC you may qualify for, and what terms may be available. The examples in this book are designed to teach how HELOCs work – but your real options can only be determined by reviewing your actual numbers.

If you would like a **no-obligation Home Equity Line of Credit review**, you can request one here:

Website: https://www.nodocsheloc.com

Email:info@FinibiMortgage.com

A licensed mortgage broker will review your information and explain what HELOC and home equity options may be available to you based on your specific situation. No cost. No pressure. No obligation.

Joseph G. Correa

About the Author

Joseph G. Correa is a licensed mortgage broker and the founder of Finibi Mortgage, a Florida-based brokerage specializing in home equity, real estate investment financing, and alternative lending strategies for homeowners, business owners, and investors. With more than two decades of experience in mortgage lending, underwriting, and financial structuring, Joseph has helped thousands of borrowers access capital using intelligent, low-risk leverage rather than high-interest consumer debt.

Unlike traditional loan officers who focus only on closing transactions, Joseph's approach is rooted in long-term financial strategy. He believes that mortgages, HELOCs, and credit lines should be used as tools for building wealth, protecting cash flow, and creating financial resilience — not as traps that keep families locked into decades of unnecessary interest payments. This philosophy has made him a trusted advisor for entrepreneurs, real estate investors, and self-employed borrowers who need flexible, modern financing solutions that banks often fail to provide.

Joseph is widely known for his expertise in home equity lines of credit, no-documentation and bank-statement loan programs, investor financing, and creative equity-based strategies such as debt-elimination systems and capital recycling. His ability to translate complex lending rules into simple, actionable guidance has helped homeowners turn idle equity into productive capital for investments, businesses, and passive income.

Through his education platform, Finibi Academy, Joseph has trained tens of thousands of students worldwide in credit, mortgage strategy, real estate financing, and financial independence. His courses and books are used by first-time homeowners, seasoned investors, and financial professionals seeking a clearer, more honest understanding of how modern lending really works.

Joseph created *The Home Equity Wealth Series* to give everyday homeowners the same financial knowledge that banks, hedge funds, and institutional investors use to control capital and minimize risk. His mission is simple: to help people stop guessing, stop fearing debt, and start using smart leverage to build real financial freedom.

When he is not structuring loans or writing, Joseph works with families and investors across the United States to design personalized equity strategies that align with their goals, cash flow, and long-term wealth plans.

The Home Equity Wealth Series Roadmap

The Professional Guide to Using Your Home to Build Financial Freedom

The purpose of *The Home Equity Wealth Series* is to give homeowners the same financial tools and strategies used by banks, investors, and institutions—translated into clear, practical guidance for everyday people. Each book builds on the last, taking you from basic understanding to advanced mastery of how to use home equity safely, intelligently, and profitably across every stage of life.

Book 1 — *HELOC Fundamentals*This book gives you the foundation. You will understand how Home Equity Lines of Credit work, how they are structured, how risk is controlled, and how equity becomes usable capital. The books that follow are designed to help you apply that knowledge to your own situation, your income type, your credit profile, and your long-term financial goals.

Book 2 — *How to Qualify for a HELOC* This book shows you how lenders actually evaluate borrowers. You will learn how credit scores, income, property type, and debt ratios affect approval, limits, and interest rates. You will also learn how to position yourself to qualify for the largest possible credit line at the best possible terms.

Book 3 — *HELOCs for Real Estate Investors* This book focuses on using home equity to buy, rehab, refinance, and scale rental properties. It explains how investors use HELOCs for down payments, renovations, and portfolio growth while keeping cash flow positive and risk controlled.

Book 4 — *Self-Employed HELOC Strategies* Designed for business owners, freelancers, 1099 borrowers, and LLCs, this book explains how bank-statement income, business income, and alternative documentation can be used to qualify for home equity even when traditional tax returns do not reflect true cash flow.

Book 5 — *Credit Mastery for HELOC Approval* This book dives deep into credit strategy. You will learn how utilization, credit mix, and reporting behavior affect HELOC limits and pricing—and how to optimize your credit profile specifically for home equity approval.

Book 6 — *No-Doc & Alternative HELOC Programs* This book covers asset-based HELOCs, no-income-verification options, and non-traditional lending programs for high-net-worth, self-employed, or cash-heavy borrowers who do not fit inside standard underwriting models.

Book 7 — *Using a HELOC to Eliminate Debt* This book teaches how to use home equity to replace high-interest credit cards, personal loans, and auto loans with low-interest revolving credit, allowing borrowers to eliminate debt years faster and save tens of thousands of dollars in interest.

Book 8 — *Using a HELOC to Build Wealth* This book shows how homeowners fund investments, businesses, and passive income streams using HELOCs while maintaining liquidity and controlling risk.

Book 9 — *HELOC Risk Management* This book focuses entirely on safety. You will learn how to structure buffers, cash-flow coverage, rate protection, and leverage limits so your home becomes safer over time—not more vulnerable.

Book 10 — *The Smart Borrower's Home Equity Blueprint* The final book ties everything together into a complete lifetime strategy for using home equity as a personal banking system, investment engine, and financial safety net.

Book 11 — *The Cashflow Accelerator Method*

The Cashflow Accelerator Method is the final transformation stage of *The Home Equity Wealth Series*. While the earlier books teach how to access, qualify for, and safely use home equity, this book teaches how to **weaponize cash flow itself** to permanently eliminate debt and create lasting wealth.

Together, these books are designed to turn a single asset—your home—into a lifelong financial advantage. Each volume adds another layer of understanding, allowing you to move from homeowner to capital manager, from borrower to strategist, and from financial stress to long-term stability.

This is not about taking more risk.It is about learning how money really works—and using that knowledge to build financial freedom that lasts.

Educational & Financial Disclaimer

This book is provided for **educational and informational purposes only**. The author and publisher are not engaged in rendering legal, tax, accounting, investment, or financial advice. Although the author is a licensed mortgage broker, the information in this book is intended to provide general education about Home Equity Lines of Credit (HELOCs) and home equity strategy, not personalized financial, legal, or lending advice.

Mortgage programs, underwriting guidelines, interest rates, credit requirements, and home equity products vary by lender, investor, state, and economic conditions, and may change at any time without notice. The examples, calculations, and scenarios presented in this book are hypothetical and are for illustration only. They do not represent guaranteed outcomes or actual loan approvals.

Before making any financial decisions, including applying for a HELOC, refinancing, borrowing against home equity, or using credit for investment or debt repayment, readers should consult with a qualified mortgage professional, financial advisor, tax advisor, or attorney who can evaluate their specific situation.

Risk Disclosure

Borrowing against home equity involves risk. A HELOC is secured by your home, which means failure to make required payments could result in foreclosure or loss of property. This book teaches responsible, conservative, and structured use of home equity, but no financial strategy is risk-free.

Readers are solely responsible for their financial decisions. Neither the author nor the publisher makes any warranties, express or implied, about the accuracy, completeness, or applicability of the information in this book to any individual or situation.

www.ingramcontent.com/pod-product-compliance
Ingram Content Group UK Ltd.
Pitfield, Milton Keynes, MK11 3LW, UK
UKHW020156290926
15471UKWH00005B/913

9 798295 573859